Mother mountain lion and three cubs, Miller Butte, National Elk Refuge, Jackson, Wyoming

Spirit of the Rockies
The Mountain Lions of Jackson Hole

To Michelle — Great meeting you. Enjoy

THOMAS D. MANGELSEN
story by Cara Shea Blessley

the mountain lions of Miller Butte. Best wishes — Th Mangelsen Oct 2000

Mountain lion watchers, National Elk Refuge

Introduction

Indian Summer, 1999. The high peaks of the Tetons are covered with their first dusting of snow. A magpie lands on the wooden wheels of the old wagon outside my window and an osprey circles above, eyeing the pond full of cutthroat trout laying in the deep, clear, cold water. Last night there was a heavy frost; the colors of the cottonwoods along the Snake are muted now but the red, burnt gold, and green leaves of the aspens hold on, quivering on a southern breeze. ∞ This day my imaginings turn to a family of mountain lions east of here high on a ridge in the Gros Ventres intently watching a herd of elk grazing in a meadow below. Towards evening the family will make their way quietly through the dim spruce forest and wait until darkness falls. The sound of bugling elk will echo through the valley. Distracted by the rut, the mountain lions will have a momentary advantage. ∞ On the evening of February 14th, 1999, I received the best Valentine's Day present ever – a call from a friend that had seen a family of mountain lions on Miller Butte inside the National Elk Refuge not far from my home. I had never seen a wild mountain lion before, and after spending nearly all my life in the field, I was not optimistic I ever would. This indeed was a rare opportunity. The next morning I awoke early, an hour before daybreak, and drove the fifteen miles to Miller Butte. It was just getting light when I arrived. Below Miller Butte, a hundred yards away I could see the shadowy figure of a large cat heading uphill. It was one of the cubs and it disappeared into a cave. I couldn't believe my eyes, my first mountain lion. ∞ During the next 42 days I spent nearly all of my time observing and photographing one of the most extraordinary wildlife events of my life. I was not alone; hundreds of people from the community and visitors from far away came to see the family of cougars. They were armed not with guns but with binoculars, spotting scopes, telescopes, still cameras, video and movie cameras. ∞ I had pretty much resigned myself to the fact that I would never make an image of a mountain lion, since nearly all photographs of mountain lions were of captive trained animals from "game farms" – places where people go to photograph a menagerie of genetically wild animals kept in cages and placed in natural surroundings for photographers and filmmakers. Many game farms have sprung up from the belief, and the excuse, that wild predators, especially mountain lions and wolves, are so rare that they could only be photographed by using animals kept in captivity. I've always believed given enough time, patience, and luck there is not an animal, at least in North America, that could not be photographed in the wild. The serendipitous events of the family of mountain lions arriving and staying on Miller Butte is a testament to that. I feel blessed and so fortunate not only to have seen and observed them but also to have been able to photograph them. The distances were far, one hundred yards or more using lenses of 600mm and 800mm and with extenders reaching over 2,200 mm, which needed to be braced using two tripods. The blowing snow, long distances, harsh winds, and the fact that the lions were usually only active during early morning and late evening, made this one of the more technically-challenging situations I've been in. ∞ The three cubs, a male and two females – now fourteen months old – are nearly full grown and ready to be on their own. The coming winter will be challenging. Their mother will have taught them well on how to survive in the wild. But, the greatest danger they will face she will not be able to pass on. Mountain lion hunting season has already begun and there is more pressure on her family this year than last. The hunting quota for mountain lions in her family's territory has more than doubled since last fall – from five to twelve animals. ∞ So it is, that one of the most historical events in mountain lion history may never be repeated. More than a thousand men, women, and children were permanently touched by this family of mountain lions. For 42 days they gave us a glimpse into their lives as no other wild mountain lions have done before. They tolerated our presence in their home. We owe not only this family of cougars but the species as a whole a more tolerant view of them. I learned much about what it means to be wild in those days on the refuge and will be eternally grateful to the mountain lions of Miller Butte for giving me such a gift.

Tom Mangelsen, September 29, 1999

U nder the shadow of the Teton Range in western Wyoming lies a landscape that is enchanting to both residents and visitors alike. Few places in North America are home to such a varied and astonishing array of wild things. Bison still roam the valley of Jackson Hole year-round. Pronghorn antelope can be spotted throughout the lower ranges of the Gros Ventre mountains, their pale rumps giving away their presence among the silvery green sage flats. Mule deer graze on high buttes, hidden against rocky outcroppings. And there, nestled between the Gros Ventre and Teton mountain ranges, sits the National Elk Refuge, home to the largest concentration of wintering elk on the continent. ∽ As the sun rises higher and higher in the crisp winter sky, light bathes the 13,770 foot Grand Teton one foot at a time. Fix your eye to its peak and you can watch the light move, bringing the valley to life in slow motion Technicolor, marking the end of another long, frozen night. *February 14, 1999*: a Sunday morning, and St. Valentine's Day. On top of Miller Butte, a solitary feline figure ghosts her way across the ridge, ears pricked forward, taking in every movement on the National Elk Refuge below. By the time the sun is up, she has disappeared into a crevice in the rocks. Glancing up at Miller Butte, you'd never know she was there. ∽ A female mountain lion with three seven-month old cubs has moved her family to a south-facing cave, one that is early to get light and offers a perfect vantage point over the land that stretches out beneath them. Of the two adjacent caves on the butte, the mother chooses the higher and slightly more concealed one. A tuft of frozen, yellowed wild rye grass blurs the entrance, making it hard to tell whether or not the lions are inside. If you can figure out where to look, their white muzzles are the only distinguishing feature of their presence in the new den site. For the next 42 days, this will be her family's home. ∽ Word of the mountain lion family on the National Elk Refuge spread quickly through the valley of Jackson Hole. An outpost of Western Americana, Jackson attracts more than 3 million visitors annually making the pilgrimage to Grand Teton and Yellowstone National Parks. With a population of nearly 5,000 permanent residents, the community takes special interest in the valley's diversity of wildlife and accessibility to outdoor activities. News of the mountain lion family and the recent arrival of wolves from Yellowstone

Mountain lion cub leaving main den
left: *Miller Butte and caves*

13

Cub on Miller Butte

left: Three lion cubs at den entrance

Three cubs climbing Miller Butte

had naturalists, photographers, tourists, and locals flocking to view the newcomers. Upon hearing news of the lion family, avid wildlife watchers from other states made a special visit, intrigued by the opportunity to see a mountain lion in the wild. A posted sign stating "Parking for Mountain Lions" directed traffic to a specially-plowed parking lot on the Elk Refuge Road. In spite of below-zero temperatures, legions of people came out to see the cats. By the end of the first week, more than three hundred people had flooded the National Elk Refuge to get a glimpse of the mother lion and her three cubs. ∞ Resident biologists on the National Elk Refuge documented the arrival of the female lion on February 12th, 1999 by a cow elk kill that was clearly made by a mountain lion. When a refuge biologist went out to examine the predated animal and the tell-tale drag marks in the snow, he turned to see the mother mountain lion standing there, no more than one hundred yards away. It was not until she made her way to the den on Miller Butte on February 14th that they realized she was a mother cougar with three cubs in tow. ∞ In all likelihood, this is the same female mountain lion that was recorded on the National Elk Refuge from December of 1994 to mid-March, 1995. She had two cubs, but was seen near the same cave on Miller Butte only twice. This time, four years later, she has a new litter of cubs. At seven-months old they are beginning to lose the dark spots they were born with, part of nature's design intended to camouflage the young cats at the most vulnerable stage of their life. Against the dappled patterns of snow upon rock, the cubs seem to vanish. ∞ Female lions move their cubs often, choosing concealed dens among rocks, in caves, or under heavy brush. Approximately every five to six days, the mother lion would transfer her cubs to either another location on Miller Butte or into the adjacent Bridger-Teton National forest to the east. Every time she disappeared – at least nine times over the course of the 42 days – the throngs of people observing the family held their breath, fearing she had abandoned the cave on Miller Butte for good. What she was doing, in fact, was moving her family for short intervals, perhaps to be nearer to her kills. ∞ The proximity of the lions' cave to the abundant elk below made the cliffside den an attractive option for the mother cat. The most common food source of mountain lions is both white-tailed and mule deer, but here in the northern Rockies, the large prey base of elk makes up the bulk of this family's diet. At this crucial stage in their lives, the female leaves her cubs behind while she hunts, caching them in the cave for hours at a time. ∞ The National Elk Refuge was established in 1912 as a response measure to the growing number of elk dying from lack of food. As the valley of Jackson Hole was settled in the early-1900s, domestic livestock brought in by homesteaders and ranchers depleted the scant vegetation, and soon the elk were competing with the cattle for the sparse forage. With the encouragement of locals, the U.S. Fish and Wildlife Service intervened and Congress established the managed winter range and feeding program that is still in effect today. Today, the refuge provides forage for roughly 7,500 animals, the management objective for the wintering elk population. If grasses are not

Mountain lion cubs on National Elk Refuge

Elk herd, National Elk Refuge

accessible because of heavy snows, the feeding program is implemented, on average, for two and a half months, from late-January to the first of April. For the last twelve years, the number of elk on the refuge have exceeded the management objective, with the winter of 1996 setting a record with over 11,000 elk. Since the summer range of these same animals stretches to the shores of Yellowstone Lake, it is not surprising that come winter, elk overcrowd the 24,700 acre refuge, the smallest piece of federal public land in Jackson Hole. ∞ In the wee morning hours the mother lion comes back for her cubs, leading them to a kill she has made on the steep grade of Miller Butte. Mountain lions are crepuscular, so the majority of their activity takes place just before dawn or right after sunset, when the light is low. It is at this time that the mother lion takes her cubs to the kills, where they feed on fresh meat to nourish their rapidly-growing bodies. Before daybreak, they return to the safety of their den, bedding down for most of the day. ∞ During the first seven days on the refuge, the mother lion made one kill every night, all in different locations. Biologists on the refuge deduced that she had been in dire straits and very hungry when she arrived, and with coyotes moving in on her kills, it simply behooved her to hunt again. After the first week, the female averaged one kill every four days. Shortly after her arrival the refuge began its managed feeding program, drawing elk off Miller Butte and out of the surrounding forested areas. This factor affected her kill rate as she tended to avoid the flats below, limiting her hunting areas to the hillsides of Miller Butte. ∞ Hunting elk is a uniquely learned behavior in mountain lions, which are usually more

adept at taking the smaller mule- and white-tailed deer. Mountain lions can take healthy, full grown deer and elk, but like all predators they are opportunistic and will concentrate their efforts on sick, weak, or immobile prey. Field biologists are able to determine the health of a predated animal by examining the bone marrow of its carcass. The bone marrow is essentially a fat reserve, and the presence of a red, gelatinous matter indicates the animal will soon die of starvation. Cases in which the marrow looks like strawberry jelly – versus the consistency of white vegetable shortening indicative of a healthy animal – shows that the predator is taking sick animals, weeding out the weak members of the population. Of the twenty-six animals that the female lion preyed on in 1995 while living on the refuge, bone marrow identifications showed seventy-five percent to be animals with depleted fat reserves on the verge of starvation. As the natural balance of a predator-prey relationship is restored, the gene pool of future elk herds will be strengthened, translating to an overall healthier population of animals. ∞ Kevin Painter, outdoor recreation planner of the National Elk Refuge, describes this area as the "fish bowl of wildlife viewing in Jackson Hole." The nine wolves that arrived in the winter of 1999 signified an important milestone in the history of Jackson Hole. Not since 1934 had a wolf been documented on the National Elk Refuge. It was not surprising, nor was it unexpected that the offspring of the wolves reintroduced to Yellowstone National Park in 1995 would eventually make their way down into the valley of Jackson Hole. The tremendous number of animals concentrated in a relatively small area of land, combined with the fact that the elk are virtually naive to being pursued by wolves, long absent from the ecosystem, made hunting elk on the refuge an easier matter. ∞ The nine wolves documented on the refuge during the winter of 1999 were made up of animals from three separate packs. The first wolves that arrived on January 7th were three stragglers and not considered an official pack. They spent most of the winter in Jackson Hole, and were undoubtably the new stars of the National Elk Refuge. Two days later, on January 9th, a pack of six wolves was spotted and concluded to be the Soda Butte pack, intact with the exception of one male that was presumed to have struck out on his own. This pack came and went during the course of the winter,

Mountain lion family and elk kill on Miller Butte

making long treks back into Yellowstone no fewer than three times, finally returning to Yellowstone for the spring. ∾ The fractured pack of three wolves is understood to have originated from two different wolf packs. The grey wolf, a male, came from the Nez Perce pack of the Old Faithful area, while the two black wolves, both females, were yearlings from the Thorofare pack, supposedly disassembled when they encountered the Soda Butte pack near the area of Moran, south of Yellowstone National Park. This group of wolves was never named during the winter, as wolves are not considered a pack until they bear pups. Since then, however, the three wolves who spent most of the winter on the National Elk Refuge denned in the Bridger-Teton National Forest and were christened the Gros Ventre pack. ∾ Joining forces was advantageous for the three wolves. Like most members of the Canidae group (which includes all domestic breeds of dogs) wolves are pack animals that depend on the strength of numbers to make kills and provide a living for each other. They work together to bring down prey, usually picking out the injured or sickly animals, heading them off until they are separated from the rest of the herd. At that point, the wolves snap at the heels of their prey, biting and pulling at various parts of the body until eventually they bring the animal down. ∾ Carcasses fed on by wolves have a distinct appearance from those fed on by mountain lions – perhaps this is because wolves hunt collectively, as a pack. In the case of a wolf kill the site reflects chaos, with big pieces of meat pulled off in chunks with different parts of the flesh consumed at random. Mountain lion kills differ in that one portion of the carcass is fed on at a time while the rest is left intact, almost as if the prey were being methodically dissected. ∾ Cougars are meticulous when it comes to their kills. In warmer seasons, they typically drag the prey to a shaded area, burying it under branches and leaves to preserve the freshness of the meat and postpone spoilage. In the heart of winter, the mother lion may have covered her kills with snow and earth perhaps to conceal the kill and protect the meat from scavengers. ∾ As many as eight species scavenged the remains of elk taken by the wolves: Ravens, weasels, coyotes, magpies, bald- and golden eagles, and Northern harrier- and American rough-legged hawks. With their incredible sense of sight, ravens flock to kills made by wolves and mountain

Calf elk taken down by mountain lion

Wolves and raven on elk carcass
left: *Wolf and elk herd*

lions. Keen scavengers, they are also known to raid the nests of other birds and will even dare to steal trout catches from river otters and bald eagles. The coyote, while cunning and nearly as keen, may take down elk calves, mule deer fawns, and even adult deer when hunting in packs. But the bulk of the coyotes' diet consists of voles and mice, which they detect by a fine-tuned inner ear capable of sensing motion beneath the snow. Making a living in winter in the northern Rockies can be difficult for coyotes. But with the wolves and lions living and hunting on the refuge, the coyotes' diet was greatly augmented by the excess of elk carrion. ∞ In the delicate instance where mountain lions coexist with wolves, the cats will go out of their way to avoid them. Just as hounds are used to trail and tree mountain lions, so too will wolves pursue the large cats. Observations made on the National Elk Refuge point to the conclusion that the presence of the three wolves influenced the females' decision to stay in the cave on Miller Butte for an inordinately long period of time. In a number of field studies, specifically one conducted by the Hornocker Wildlife Institute in Yellowstone National Park, wolves have been recorded driving lions off kills. In addition, the wolves will often hunt and try to kill lions, threatening the lives of both the mother lion and her cubs. Leaving the den any earlier than she did may have resulted in a fatal confrontation with the three wolves. ∞ With the exception of Hugh Miles' documentation of a female mountain lion in his National Geographic Special, *Puma: Lion of the Andes*, filmed in Torres del Paine National Park in Chilean Patagonia, the situation of the mountain lion family in Jackson Hole knows no equivalent. The circumstances, in which a mountain lion family was capable of being observed for nearly six weeks, was considered by most – including seasoned naturalists and experienced cougar researchers – to be a once-in-a-lifetime situation. In no other known or documented instance – even in the case of field biologists who dedicate their lives to studying lions – has such an extended period of observation been recorded in the wild. The challenge of studying the cougar attests to the dedication of these steadfast scientists: The allure of the mountain lion lies in its elusiveness, in its nature to conceal its day-to-day habits, behaviors, and whereabouts. ∞ One of the most obvious effects of the new residents on the refuge – the wolves and mountain lions –

Wolves and ravens, National Elk Refuge

Coyote behind drifting snow
right: Coyote on Miller Butte

Coyotes scavenging elk kill made by wolves

32

was the elimination of diseased elk from the herd. While the debate continues as to whether predators can actually affect, let alone control, populations, their hunting and making a living on the refuge encourages a stronger, more disease-resistant breeding population of elk in the long run, enlightening the many discussions on how to manage the National Elk Refuge in the future. ∞ With elk numbers at a historical high in the valley of Jackson Hole, certain areas of Grand Teton National Park have been opened to the fall hunt. In spite of the Wyoming Game and Fish Department giving out as many elk licenses as possible, hunters still can't seem to significantly reduce the number of elk in Jackson Hole. Many who have purchased licenses go home without even seeing an elk in the open hunting area, let alone being within firing range of one. Biologists and hunters agree that avoiding the areas open to the fall hunt is learned behavior among the elk herds. They find places to hide and hold out in and around Blacktail Butte and other places in Grand Teton National Park, crossing the Snake River and into the closed-to-hunting area of the National Elk Refuge during the night. As a result, the hunters go home empty-handed and the elk, having outsmarted their human pursuers, go on to stretch the carrying capacity of the National Elk Refuge. ∞ While everyone has their own opinions and interests in mind on how to handle this issue – from wildlife managers to environmentalists to hunters and hunting outfitters – the obvious answer points first and foremost to restoring a natural balance of predator-to-prey. The school of thought known as deep ecology suggests that we need to live in such a way that there is space for wild creatures within our midst. This means that while we benefit from the advantage of an ecosystem complete with predators, we must also be aware, and therefore cautious, of the possible risks to humans. These include jogging at dusk on a heavily wooded trail in mountain lion habitat or the interaction resulting from leaving garbage outdoors to be discovered by curious and hungry predators, such as bears. ∞ Predators have historically been widely feared and therefore, widely misunderstood. Myths abound regarding the danger of wild creatures. One of our most popular fairy tales, told to children early on, relays the story of Little Red Riding Hood encountering "The Big Bad Wolf". Popular films such as the 1998 nature-thriller *The Edge*, starring Anthony

Hopkins, play on our collective fear of predators, boxing them into the stereotype of wild animals that look to confront, attack, and consecutively devour humans. In reality, just the opposite is true: Predators have learned that humans are the greatest threat to their survival. Taking the time to learn about and understand the habits and behaviors of animals while exercising caution and good sense can greatly diminish unfortunate interactions with mountain lions, wolves, bears, and even the giant herbivore that is the buffalo. As Wayne Pacelle, senior vice president for communications and government affairs of the Humane Society, states in his essay, *Bullets, Ballots, and Predatory Instincts,* "Deer, bees, goats and even jellyfish account for more human fatalities than mountain lions. For every person killed by a lion, 1,200 are struck by lightening and 1,100 are killed in hunting accidents." ∞ But it is the predator that captures our imaginations – we dare to feel the excitement that the unpredictable wild brings to our lives. There is undoubtedly a mystique to hiking, exploring, and living in the realm of wild things, having the possibility to not only encounter but also be affected by animals that make their homes among us. Predators are the magic of the wild: the grizzlies and coyotes, the wolves and mountain lions. ∞ Night falls over the National Elk Refuge. *March 2, 1999*: The second blue moon of the year. As the sun drops over the Grand Teton and daylight dissolves from the sky, the elk become wary, their senses heightened and alert to the danger of their new neighbors on the refuge. Darkness takes over and a group of Rocky Mountain bighorn sheep clambers to the ridge of Miller Butte, peering out into the night. Their posture – heads held erect, all eyes pointing the same direction – shows tell-tale signs of tension, a visceral reaction as the moon rolls over in the winter sky.

Rocky Mountain Bighorn Sheep on Miller Butte at dusk

preceding: Rocky Mountain Bighorn Sheep on Miller Butte at night
Bull elk and the Sleeping Indian under full moon
right: Mountain lions on Miller Butte at nightfall

Sunrise over Gros Ventre Range

40

Mountain lions hold more heritage to this land than any other predator throughout the Americas. So extensive was their range, that they once inhabited the United States from the Atlantic to the Pacific oceans, filling every suitable landscape as far north as the northernmost Canadian Rockies all the way to the southern tip of South America and Chilean Patagonia. Adaptable as they are, and must be, mountain lions have historically created a niche wherever the prey base was large enough to support their existence. This includes temperate coastal forests, vast plains, high mountain cliffsides, rocky hillside crags, and the driest of deserts throughout the West and Southwest. ∞ Lending to their mystique, mountain lions are known by, and called, more names than any other mammal. Cougar, puma, catamount ('cat of the mountain'), painter, panther, shadow cat, and ghost cat are all names that refer to *Puma concolor,* the American mountain lion. There has even been confusion regarding its Latin name. In 1993, at the suggestion of taxonomist W.C. Wozencraft, the mountain lion was reclassified from *Felis concolor* to *Puma concolor.* Previously, it was classified as a small cat, *Felis,* due to the inflexible hyoid bone at the base of its tongue and the structure of its voice box, with its tightly bound set of bones which prevents the mountain lion from being able to roar. While the cougar does have a repertoire of vocalizations, including growls, mews, squeaks, chirps, hisses, and yowls, it cannot roar like its Felidae cousins the African lion or Bengal tiger. The previous classification, however, was an arbitrary one. Given its size, weight, and skull measurements, the mountain lion is clearly a large cat, but only recently has it officially been recognized as such. ∞ Imagine a mammal that is capable of roaming such distinct and varied climates, terrains, and landscapes. Imagine the quiet steps of a neighbor's housecat stalking birds in the garden and stretch that picture to encompass a large, tawny colored cat of 75 to 150 pounds, eyes intent on its prey, each rear paw finding the placement of the forepaw that precedes it. Imagine a cliff, at first glance indistinguishable from any other. Imagine this cat, the second largest of the Americas, hiding under a rocky outcropping, watching the activity below, waiting for the moment when the sun steps down from its daytime post and falls behind the mountains. See the glow of sage green eyes, mesmerizing and intent, curious,

Mother mountain lion on rocky outcropping, Miller Butte

Cow elk migrating north, National Elk Refuge

hungry, alive. Imagine the slow pulse of the cat as she waits for the precise moment to descend upon her prey, the concentration, the split second before intent materializes into motion. ∞ The sun rises, breathing life into the birds, animals and budding plants of Jackson Hole. The heat of the day is noticeably stronger, the chill snap of early spring giving way to warm rays of sun filling the cliffside den of the mountain lion family. Suddenly, winter seems only a memory. ∞ With a few days of sunshine and temperatures peaking at forty-degrees, the snow melts away in patches, revealing dark earth, latent with possibilities of wildflowers and new meadow grasses. This is the elks' cue, and they begin to disperse, so gradually as to be almost imperceptible. Traveling at all times of the day and night, they head up into the neighboring Bridger-Teton National Forest, advancing north along the sage flats, past Blacktail Butte and into the heart of Grand Teton National Park. Along the way they graze on grasses of the previous fall exposed by melting snow, nipping sparse new plant growth as they travel. The elk move in waves, sensitive to weather patterns and inclement storms. When the possibility of snow threatens their journey to higher elevations, they retreat, tuning their migration to atmospheric conditions. The once-numerous, condensed elk herd is now spread out over the valley of Jackson Hole. ∞ With the elk go the wolves, as their main prey clears out to high mountain meadows where they will calve and raise their young near abundant food in protected forest clearings. The Soda Butte

Mother lion in main den, Miller Butte

Mother mountain lion and female cub in main den, Miller Butte

Male and female cub in adjacent den, Miller Butte

pack has returned to Yellowstone National Park, and the newly-named Gros Ventre pack has headed up into the Bridger-Teton National Forest to choose a denning site for their first litter of pups. ∞ The mountain lion cubs, too, feel the warmth of the new day, the start of a new season. They embody the jubilant nature of springtime, taking turns pouncing on one another and batting a piece of elk hide carried away from a kill to be used as a plaything. The little male mock-stalks the first mountain bluebirds of the year, their flash of color brightening the lichen-covered cliffs of Miller Butte. A prairie falcon, having just arrived from farther south, perches on a rock ledge, considering the steep cliffs of Miller Butte as an ideal nest site for her coming brood. A pair of golden eagles has the same idea, and secures their pair bond in a beautiful dance above the butte, tumbling and falling, taking turns playing chase against the brilliant azure backdrop of a cloudless spring sky. ∞ The mountain lion family's interest is peaked by all the movement below. They take it in, the mother lion calculating her family's departure with the timing of the other animals on the refuge. The den on Miller Butte has become a safe-haven for her family. While the people on the Elk Refuge Road below were never the cause of any unrest, outside of the context of her den on Miller Butte, she knows better. ∞ Mountain lions evolved to escape from their sole predator, the wolf, tens of thousands of years ago, when the two roamed and competed on the uninhabited North American landscape. With retract-able claws, lions can pad silently through a forest littered with pine needles and crinkling leaves. The same feature allows them to scale trees, climbing up and away from danger. The mountain lion of today – genetically tuned for fleeing from wolves – has not evolved the instinct to keep running when being chased by dogs, nor has it learned to anticipate that its main predator is now human. ∞ Four months after the arrival of the mountain lion family on the National Elk Refuge, the annual Wyoming limit for the 1999-2000 mountain lion hunt went up for review. In spite of letters documenting the lack of concrete proof that lion numbers had increased, The Wyoming Game and Fish Department raised the quota from five to twelve animals in Area 2-Teton, which includes the valley of Jackson Hole. Beginning "where the Continental Divide crosses the southern boundary of Yellowstone National Park", it encompasses the Bridger-Teton

Mother mountain lion and two cubs playing with elk hide

Wilderness in the Gros Ventre range, south to the Hoback Rim, along the westerly border of the Snake River beginning at Dry Wash Draw to the Wyoming-Idaho border, and north again to the Continental Divide: In effect, the home range of the mother lion and her three cubs. ∞ In a newspaper article announcing the proposed expansion of lion hunting in Wyoming, the opening quote from a Wyoming Game and Fish Department official stated that "it is virtually impossible to get an accurate count of an actual lion population" (Pinedale Roundup, June 19, 1999). Yet a source that wishes to remain unnamed at the Regional Office in Jackson, Wyoming, claimed that the limit was raised due to "an increase in lion sightings, more human-lion conflict, and from counts established by overhead flight and field surveys." ∞ Counts of mountain lions in the twelve western states combined range between 10,000 to 50,000. Lion populations are notably so difficult to determine mainly because the big cats are so elusive and patrol home ranges up to 150 square miles. Presently, mountain lions are known to have viable breeding populations – cases in which there exists at least 250 animals of each sex for at least one hundred years – in twelve western states: Utah, Wyoming, Colorado, Montana, Idaho, Arizona, New Mexico, Nevada, Texas, Washington, Oregon, and California. The situation of mountain lions in the east is bleak. Although there have been scattered sightings, a number of them in the Appalachian mountains, there is no solid proof that mountain lions still occur in the eastern United States. In Florida, the subspecies *Puma concolor coryi* is just barely hanging on, with a mere 30-50 animals known to remain. ∞ With the exception of Texas and California, all states with mountain lion populations have regulated seasons and limits on lion hunting. In Texas, hunters may shoot as many lions as they can find – there is no restriction on lion hunting whatsoever. In California, the converse is true: In 1990, the mountain lion was reclassified from a game animal to be hunted to an animal to be protected. Those involved in monitoring lion hunting and legislation of hunting laws attribute the support of this decision to an extensive public education program administered on behalf of the California Department of Fish and Game, resulting in a greater awareness and knowledge of the mountain lion. ∞ Why then, given such overwhelming evidence as to the inaccuracy of mountain lion counts, did the Wyoming

Game and Fish Department increase the quotas for Area 2-Teton? Even given the reasons WGFD stated, did they not consider the reasonable answers? Could an increase in lion sightings have anything to do with the fact that more and more people are venturing out into wilderness areas? Could an increase in human-lion conflict (a word which is often inappropriately used to define *interaction*) be a result of human encroachment – in the form of suburbs and residential development – into wilderness areas and into the habitats of mountain lions? And in spite of the increases in lion sightings and in human-lion "conflict", the Bozeman, Montana-based *Predator Conservation Alliance* states that they "have heard of no incidents of lions injuring people in Wyoming, even in Jackson where many people took advantage of a rare opportunity to view a female lion and her kittens this past spring." ∞ Removal of the lion from bountied predator to game status in all states in the West, except Texas, was a huge victory for the mountain lion. However, the sport of mountain lion trophy hunting continues to be an issue that challenges the ethics of true sportsmen – even many big game hunters have a difficult time coming to terms with hunting mountain lions. While elk provide a viable food source for the hunter, hunting a mountain lion is simply a matter of killing an animal to obtain its skin, or stuffed body, as a trophy. ∞ In considering the amount of joy derived from observing a rare animal in its natural habitat, in which circumstance does the experience of the mountain lion go farther? In the case of the mountain lions of Jackson Hole, in which an entire community relished in the chance to observe an elusive cougar? Or in the instance where the experience is used up for the enjoyment of only one person – the trophy hunter who gets to pull the trigger on the big cat? Why does the Wyoming Game and Fish Department not rally to preserve its mountain lion population and instead team up with the Wyoming Tourism Board, offering an alternative to hunting outfitters who could instead take people out into the field to track, observe, and photograph mountain lions? ∞ In the case where mountain lion hunting is supported and implemented as a way to keep mountain lion populations in check and human-lion interaction to a minimum, the opposite has proven true. In Vancouver, British Colombia, the parallel has been drawn that the more lions are hunted (lion hunting is without regulation in B.C., as in

Prairie falcon roosting on rocky outcropping, Miller Butte

Mother lion and magpie on cliff, Miller Butte

Texas), the more violent and frequent are negative interactions with humans. Adult mountain lions keep their home ranges in check, which means the older lions that are more established and more experienced (versus adolescent cats still working on perfecting their hunting techniques) drive off younger cats looking to move into their territory. This form of social hierarchy among lions ensures that the areas with the most prey and best habitat are patrolled by the mature and experienced lions. When these "established" cats are killed off, it opens up the area to the often inexperienced and hungry adolescents who are more likely to seek out less challenging and more readily available prey such as domestic livestock, pets, and even people. ∞ Ken Logan, one of the nation's leading cougar field biologists, reports that "trophy hunting is by far the single greatest mortality factor for lions throughout the West." Today, many mountain lion hunts are conducted using radio-telemetry collars attached to dogs. When an outfitter comes across signs of lion activity in the brush or snow, he releases his dogs on the scent trail of the cat until eventually the lion is forced into a tree. Once treed, the hunter can shoot the cat at a near point-blank range. To make up for the lack of true sportsmanship involved, as well as to not damage their trophy hide, hunters often shoot treed lions with .22 or other small-caliber pistols, which often brings a slow and inhumane death to the animal. ∞ Even more appalling is the fact that once the cat is treed, often the client paying for the hunt is not even in the state where the hunt is taking place. In these cases, dogs may hold the lion in the tree for a number of days, an act which stresses the cat and contributes to its slow, lengthy demise. Trophy hunting is also one of the principle causes of mortality among mountain lion cubs, which when orphaned, perish without their mother. Harley Shaw, in his seminal book Soul Among Lions: The Cougar as Peaceful Adversary attests to problems with hunts of this sort: "More often than not, the guide goes along with the dogs and trees the lion, while a helper meets the client at the airport and brings him to a tree. All the client does is pull the trigger, and killing a lion in a tree is a simple matter. Such clients have not hunted lions. Stories of their hunts will be lame lies. They might just as well have bought a tanned hide from a taxidermist." ∞ With the technology available to outfitters today, and the natural instinct for

Mother mountain lion returning from hunt and waiting cub, Miller Butte

lions to tree when chased by dogs, a mountain lion hunt can be conducted virtually from the front seat of a pickup truck with a cup of coffee in hand. This is not to say that mountain lion hunts have always been this way – mountain lion trophy hunting, too, has its roots and customs, ones that are as highly-steeped in tradition as ranching is in the West. Unfortunately, many outfitters today find it too expensive to hunt lions on foot or on horseback in the more traditional, more time-consuming way. ∞ How then, to reconcile the antiquated but still sought-after experience of trophy hunting when it comes to mountain lions? Oregon and Washington, two states that still permit the hunting of lions, have banned the use of hounds in mountain lion hunts. This is a step closer to balancing the scales for both parties involved, the pursuer and the pursued; in this case, man and lion. In sporting circles, "fair chase" is the term used when the tables are relatively even for the hunter and hunted. Complying with this measure of fairness would not only make the mountain lion hunt a challenge again, but may also earn lion hunting a renewed sense of respect for all involved, the outfitter and hunter alike. ∞ Perhaps trophy hunters need to get together and redefine true sportsmanship – what is acceptable in their circles and what, simply put, is not "fair chase". If outfitters cease to profit from unethical and unsportsman-like hunts, such practices will quickly become a thing of the past. ∞ The mother mountain lion, more at ease than ever, has waited until the sun is high to return from her most recent kill. A magpie flies from rock ledge to rock ledge, following her in hopes of being led to a food cache. Around the corner of the butte, one of the mama's cubs waits for her; another hides, tucked away in a rocky crevice. The male cub, waiting in the main den, shows signs of recent interaction with a well-equipped animal: His muzzle is full of porcupine quills, evidence that honing his hunting skills comes with a risk. ∞ The days grow warmer. A pair of trumpeter swans have almost finished building their nest on Flat Creek, and the male spends part of every day driving off other swans that drift too close to their chosen site. The golden eagles, too, have settled in. Ravens turn pinwheels in the sky, their shadows laying down a kaleidoscope of patterns on the meadows below. And by now, only a few elk remain on the

southernmost edge of the refuge. For the elk and the wolves, the coming of an end to winter means that they move on. ∞ And so too, departs the family of mountain lions. As members and visitors of the community of Jackson Hole file along the Elk Refuge Road to catch one last glimpse of the mother lion and her three cubs, they realize, finally, on day number three of observation with no sign of action that she, too, has moved on. And with her, taken one of the most magical wildlife events that has ever touched this valley. Perhaps the memory of her stay here will be strong enough to encourage others to understand her species, as she disappears and resumes her existence as ghost cat, the Spirit of the Rockies.

preceding: Female lion cub hiding in rocky crevice

Mother mountain lion and sleeping cub in main den

Selected Bibliography

Busch, Robert H. *The Cougar Almanac: A Complete Natural History of the American Mountain Lion.* New York, NY: Lyons & Burford, 1996.

Craighead, Frank C. *For Everything There is a Season.* Helena: Falcon Press, 1994.

Ewing, Susan and Grossman, Elizabeth (editors). *Shadow Cat: Encountering the American Mountain Lion.* Seattle: Sasquatch Books, 1999.

Shaw, Harvey. *Soul Among Lions: The Cougar as Peaceful Adversary.* Boulder: Johnson Publishing Company, 1989.

Turner, Jack. *The Abstract Wild.* Tuscon: The University of Arizona Press, 1996.

Related Organizations

Hornocker Wildlife Institute P.O. Box 3246, Moscow, ID 83843
(208) 885-6871   www.uidaho.edu/rsrch/hwi

Mountain Lion Foundation P.O Box 1896, Sacramento, CA 95812
(916) 442-2666   www.mountainlion.org

The Rocky Mountain Elk Foundation P.O. Box 8249, Missoula, MT 59807
(800) 225-5355   www.rmef.org

The Orion Society 195 Main Street Great Barrington, MA 01230
(413) 528-4422   www.orionsociety.org

Mountain lion and New Moon, Miller Butte

The Mountain Lions of Jackson Hole